TRADITION AND EXPERIMENT
IN
MODERN SCULPTURE

Charles Seymour, Jr.

ARNO PRESS ✳ NEW YORK
A PUBLISHING AND LIBRARY SERVICE OF THE NEW YORK TIMES

ARNO SERIES OF CONTEMPORARY ART NO. 34
Reprinted with the permission of The American University
Library of Congress Catalog Card No. 70-91378
Manufactured in the United States of America
by Arno Press, New York, 1969

TRADITION
AND
EXPERIMENT
IN
MODERN SCULPTURE

by
Charles Seymour, Jr.

THE AMERICAN UNIVERSITY PRESS

Despiau   *Mme. Derain*   Original Plaster Model
The Phillips Gallery, Washington, D. C.

TRADITION
AND
EXPERIMENT
IN
MODERN SCULPTURE

By

Charles Seymour, Jr.

THE AMERICAN UNIVERSITY PRESS

1949   WASHINGTON, D. C.

Dedicated to the Memory of

C. LAW WATKINS

INTRODUCTION

"Tradition and Experiment in Modern Sculpture"—this book grew out of a recent lecture given by Charles Seymour, Jr. at The American University in which he commented upon the significance and quality of sculpture then on exhibition in The University's Watkins Gallery.

In its preparation, advantage has been taken of the opportunity to include reproductions of outstanding work in the Capital's art museums which were not available for display in the Watkins Gallery exhibition. A long-standing desire has also been fulfilled in selecting certain splendid aboriginal carvings from the archaeological and ethnological collections of the Smithsonian Institution's United States National Museum, so that they might be studied as works of art. Illustrations have been chosen where necessary from collections in other parts of the country, but emphasis remains upon resources in and around Washington. Mr. Seymour has recast and expanded the text of his lecture to meet the requirements of publication.

The Watkins Gallery in The American University is a memorial to C. Law Watkins, whose sensitivity and understanding helped nurture the art activity we observe in Washington today. Through the exhibitions in this Gallery, the University performs the essential function of familiarizing students and the interested public with original works of art. It is the premise of the Department of Fine Arts that contemporary work is most likely to be of value when it not only adds to, but also grows from, the discoveries of preceeding cultures. We believe that art is a central human activity and that the University gains from the presence of art in the curriculum, just as the student of art gains from his contact with other forms of training within the course of general humanistic studies. This book, published with the hope of encouraging awareness and understanding, is designed to suggest the implications of our approach, both intellectual and creative, to the problem of education.

Neither the book nor the first exhibition would have been possible without the splendid cooperation and generosity of many institutions and private collectors who have made their treasures available.

We wish to express our sincere thanks to Mr. Charles Seymour, Jr. not only for his contribution of the text but for his continuing enthusiasm and cooperation in the preparation of this book; to Dr. Paul F. Douglass, the President of The American University whose imagination has fostered the growth of the creative arts within a university and has now made this publication possible; to Mr. Kurt Wiener who, we feel, could not have produced a book of such handsome appearance without a love for his craft and this task in particular or without his knowledge and taste; to Mr. Victor Amato and Mr. Henry B. Beville of The National Gallery of Art, who have cooperated patiently in the endeavor to produce new photographs of many of the pieces reproduced; to Miss Barbara Burton who has cheerfully assumed the burden of checking data and countless other details; and to Miss Alice Atema of The National Gallery of Art, who was always helpful in providing photographs and information. Grateful acknowledgement is made to Mr. and Mrs. Walter C. Arensberg, Hollywood, Cal.; the Hon. and Mrs. Francis Biddle, Washington, D. C.; the Hon. Robert Woods Bliss, Washington, D. C.; Mrs. Edward Bruce, Washington, D. C.; Mr. C. S. Gulbenkian, Lisbon; Mr. and Mrs. Andrew S. Keck, Washington, D. C.; The Baltimore Museum of Art, Baltimore, Md.; The Corcoran Gallery of Art, Washington, D. C.; Musée Rodin, Paris; Musée de Versailles, Versailles; The National Gallery of Art, Washington, D. C.; The Phillips Gallery, Washington, D. C.; Smithsonian Institution, Freer Gallery of Art, and United States National Museum, Washington, D. C.; Walters Art Gallery, Baltimore, Md.; Buchholz Gallery, New York; Egan Gallery, New York; Willard Gallery, New York.

William H. Calfee
Chairman, Department of Fine Arts
The American University

Human Mask. Mexican Highland, c.1000. Serpentine
Robert Woods Bliss Collection   Courtesy National Gallery of Art

TWO

TRADITION AND EXPERIMENT IN MODERN SCULPTURE

Western civilization has developed verbal thinking further than any other. None of us is immune by training and intellectual inheritance from its influence. Much of the mystery and lack of understanding, the so-called "cultural lag" between popular appreciation and experimental work in contemporary sculpture, is due to overwhelming education in a conceptual language of words and signs and to corresponding forgetting of a language of plastic forms.

Sculpture is a language of forms. Sculpture exists in three dimensions in our own physical space and is defined not only by the space which surrounds it and that which it displaces, but by the physical light of the sun or man-made equivalents of sunlight. Whether minute miniature jewelry or a marble colossus, whether representational or abstract, whether Greek, Gothic, Mexican, Chinese, Micronesian or Modern European or American, sculpture exists first of all as a tangible reality in the physical reality of light and space. Sculpture shares the space which we breathe as air and move about in and live in. It shares the light we use to see with, more frequently than not, the same light that defines the rough bark of trees or the craggy mass of mountains. From these fundamental defining facts derive a great number of phenomena which further define sculpture. They might best be approached through what could be called the "poetics" of that art, a superstructure of values based on the realism of sculpture's tangible and visible existence.

If we are agreed that communication can be made through forms in art and that language is not restricted to words, there should be no

Water Goddess. Mexican, Aztec, c.1450-1500. Basalt
Robert Woods Bliss Collection   Courtesy National Gallery of Art

FOUR

Water Goddess. Back view of opposite plate
Robert Woods Bliss Collection   Courtesy National Gallery of Art

reason to restrict notions of poetry to literature. There is a poetry in the language of art. It is time we recognized that fact, particularly for sculpture; far too many people attempt to read sculpture as if it were a kind of prose, and too many platitudinous or dreary monuments in public places have been produced in the same spirit.

Head of Horse. Gilded Bronze   Roman, II century
Walters Art Gallery, Baltimore

THE POETICS OF SCULPTURE

The poetics of sculpture, based on formal characteristics of the art, require a willingness to look on sculpture and aesthetics with a somewhat fresh eye. In considering sculpture, I am naturally drawn into a verbal approach, but at the same time I feel a need to move outside the logical procedure of verbal prose discourse. Sculpture exists first of all as three-dimensional form. No word or combination of words can completely describe these forms or in any real way become precise equivalents for their elements. If I see sculpture as plastic form, it is not easy to consider its effects in terms of prose which demands above all, in critical writing, clarity and precision in the use of signs and their referents and seems to impose, in the very act of exposition, a similar precision of meaning on the subject matter, regardless of its nature. This difficulty can best be met by direct attack. It is very possible, if not probable, that the poetry of sculpture depends, much as some critics have shown for the poetry of literature, not upon clarity of meaning but upon ambiguity and the tensions arising therefrom.*

Sculpture is notoriously difficult to define. This is largely because much of the essence of its worth, its poetic capabilities, are inherently and inescapably dependent on unclear shifting values between two or more points or poles of meaning. In speaking of these values, we are more or less forced to consider the divergent poles of meaning in order to suggest the poetic field of ambiguity between them. Let me illustrate this idea, with several examples, as a desirable foundation for more specific analysis of recent developments in Western sculpture.

---

*In this application of literary theory to visual art, it is axiomatic, as Henri Focillon insisted in his writing and lectures, that forms in art are not to be confused with visual or verbal signs, which, of course, under certain circumstances contain strong poetical capabilities of ambiguity; forms in art, however, are different in that they are objects or parts of objects—they "signify," not something else, but themselves alone. The modern position on the nature of poetry is suggestive and bears directly on this fundamental problem in the criticism of art, for example: "The empire of prose is signs . . . the poetic attitude considers words as things and not as signs" (J. P. Sartre, *What is Literature?* New York, Philosophical Library, 1949).

Gold and Ivory Goddess. Crete, about 1600 B.C.
Walters Art Gallery, Baltimore

EIGHT

**Bronze Ceremonial Covered Vessel.   Chinese, XII century B.C. (Detail)
Courtesy Smithsonian Institution, Freer Gallery of Art, Washington, D. C.**

Although sculpture exists as solid, tangible form in real space and real air and is defined by real light, it is not by any means a passive visitor to our world of human living and human action.   It can exert a positive action of its own.   It hovers between the poles of passivity and activity in this respect.   Sculpture is both defined by space and defines space, and is both defined by light and defines light.

The phase of active definition needs, perhaps, the greater emphasis.   As a very influential modern historian of art, Henri Focillon,* has

---

*See in particular his *Life of Forms in Art*, Yale University Press, 1942; New York, Wittenborn, 1947 (translation by G. A. Kubler and C. B. Hogan), "Forms in the Realm of Space," *passim.*

A Bodhisattva. Stone, Chinese, VII century.
Courtesy Smithsonian Institution, Freer Gallery of Art, Washington, D. C.

TEN

shown, sculpture may affect our sense impressions, and in subtle ways actually defines the quality of space and light by which the form is surrounded. For example, simple contours and smooth compact surfaces define light as broad and calm and the atmosphere around them as heavy and quiescent. Deeply undercut and irregular forms on the other hand, tend to define light as a flickering movement and the atmosphere as a restless force searching like a fluid to penetrate matter, to enter through crevices and crannies the very stone or bronze itself. In the first example space is defined as a limit, virtually a solid in its own right; in the 17th-century Baroque as a porous, yielding medium for activity.

One can add a further set of oppositions in considering the factor of time. Sculpture is defined by time and also defines time. It is defined by the chronological time surrounding the fact of its creation and implied by the very resistance of its materials; it is also defined by the chronological time required by the observer to view it satisfactorily in space. Yet sculpture also defines a kind of time that is apparently independent of the clock and the seasons. Sculpture may produce impressions of great rapidity in the passage of time or of a slow beat that seems to lengthen almost to a standstill approaching the timelessness of eternity; in this sense sculpture measures a new kind of time.* Or again, the movement of a design in sculpture may represent a moment in a continuous action; yet the actual forms so used, except for certain rather rare mobile forms, are perpetually still.

Between such poles upon which definite values of meaning may be placed lie extensive fields of expression and suggestion. Here sculp-

---

*An easily recognized example is found in monumental Egyptian sculpture. I cannot believe that the particular impression of very slow moving time, virtually timelessness, arising from that art is read into the sculpture from what is known from written texts about Egyptian religion. On the contrary, it seems possible that very nearly the precise values of time in Egyptian religion could be deduced from the sculptural forms alone. For a recent analysis of this phenomenon of time, including several aspects of sculpture, see E. Souriau, "Time in the Plastic Arts," *Journal of Aesthetics*, VII, 1949, pp. 294-307. Some of these ideas in another context were published in *The Columbus Gallery of Fine Arts Bulletin, Summer, 1949.*

ture assumes new and various and poetic aspects of existence, never removed from the action of natural laws, yet at the same time playing upon those laws and creating positive interpretations of our physical environment.

Within the frame of reference of the arts, sculpture stands somewhere between architecture and painting. On the one hand it deals with stable forms in physical space as does architecture; on the other, it is available for representation and symbolism may become what the older Humanist critics called an "art of imitation"—as may painting. This double relationship with architecture and painting is of great importance in the historical development of sculpture, particularly in the Western world. But for the moment it is sufficient to emphasize that the double relationship sets up once again two poles of formal meaning: the one based on abstract solid forms in space—as in architecture—and the other on representation of objects or beings, frequently with related symbolic values. Both are important. Today we might tend to stress the importance of the first, or abstract pole. But we should not overlook the representational and symbolic end of the scale, for it in turn is a productive source of poetic power based on the two opposite poles of art and human life.

How deeply the ambiguity between these opposites has affected thought, and why to some extent it still colors our approach to sculpture, is vividly shown by the creation myths of many cultures. In effect these myths proclaim the extraordinary but very widespread belief that if man creates sculpture, he is also created by a divine sculptor, and that living man himself is a kind of sculpture in his origin.

High up on the North transept portal of Chartres Cathedral there is a brief drama in stone sometimes lost or forgotten in the unending richness of the Cathedral. The scene contains two figures, one nude and terminating at the waist in a shapeless mass, the other draped. This is the Genesis scene of the Creation of Man carved about 1240 in our era. As the Almighty bends over his labor his attitude might be mistaken for one

A Deified Queen.   Bronze, South Indian, late XI or early XII century
Courtesy Smithsonian Institution, Freer Gallery of Art, Washington, D. C.

THIRTEEN

Two Yaksi Figures. Sandstone, Indian, VIII century
The Baltimore Museum of Art

FOURTEEN

of benediction. But the pose of His hands and the action of His fingers, wrists and arms are actually intended to simulate those of a capable artist making an image, just as the Biblical text suggests—as if He were at midpoint in modeling the first man from clay. Paleolithic figures modeled from clay and pulverized bone are in fact among the first evidence of man's artistic activity on the theme of the human body. Significantly, there is no older theme than the human figure known in sculpture.

The sculptural creation myth appears very early in a modified form in Egypt, where Ammon-Ra was called "the fashioner of men." It appears in the mythology of tribes in both Atlantic and Pacific cultures and in Greek mythology, where Prometheus is described as forming the first man from earth. As a matter of history, it is probable that the Chartres sculptor imitated an ancient Prometheus relief, possibly on a Roman or Gallo-Roman sarcophagus, when he composed his group.*

With these examples in mind, the sentimental fallacy confusing living human forms with forms of sculpture is not difficult to understand. The aesthetic difficulties arising from this ambiguity are none the less real. They have clouded the critical theories about European sculpture in particular, largely because a poetic ambiguity has been confused in some catastrophic way with aesthetic requirements. There are alive today a number of people who claim to dislike a given piece of sculpture because it is not "life-like," that is to say, because it does not imitate closely enough the human body. Somewhere behind this view are age-old imaginations, the survival of older confusions between art and life like that recorded in the myth of the ivory woman by Pygmalion, which "came to life."

There appears to be a mysterious life in sculpture. But we see it as inherent in the forms as they are designed and executed by a sensitive

*See for one type of the classical motive c. 400 (Early Christian) a relief in the Lateran Museum, Rome; reproduced by Adelheid Heimann in *Journal of the Warburg Institute*, II, 1938, pl. 4. In a recent carving called *Prometheus*, illustrated here, Brancusi seems to recall this myth, suggesting the moment when man's features were just beginning to emerge under the "sculptor's magical hand.

FIFTEEN

The Courtier Bes. Egyptian, Saite Period (Detail). Limestone
C. S. Gulbenkian Collection   Courtesy National Gallery of Art

SIXTEEN

and creative artist. This life depends neither on the act of infusing a magical power into a fetish nor on imitation of natural appearances. The most accurate imitation, a cast from a life-form, the mask, for example, taken from the features of a living man can be, and generally is, dead —as sculpture.

Brancusi *Prometheus* Marble
Louise and Walter Arensberg Collection, Hollywood, California

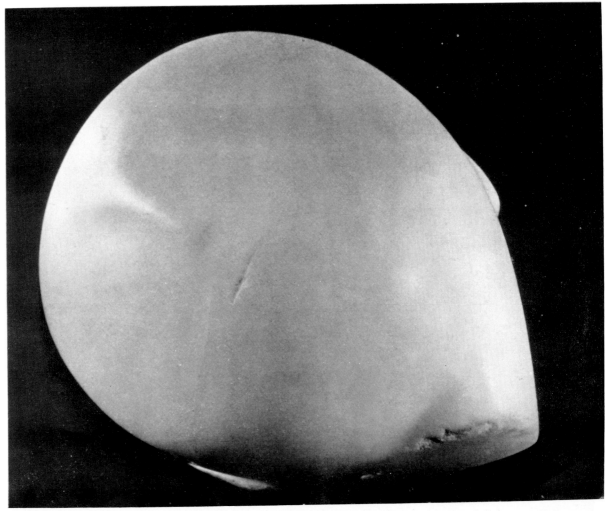

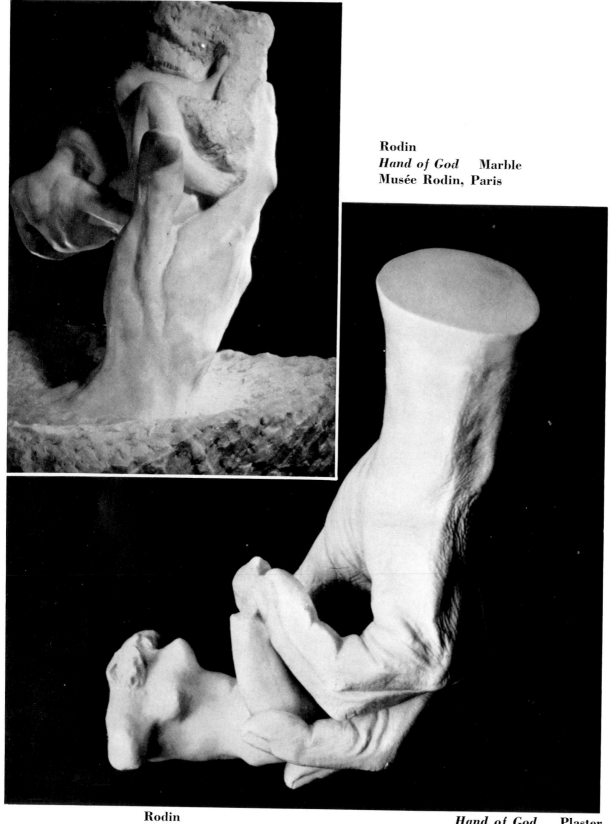

Rodin
Hand of God   Marble
Musée Rodin, Paris

Rodin   *Hand of God*   Plaster
Courtesy National Gallery of Art, Washington, D. C.

EIGHTEEN

Rodin may at one time have deliberately attempted to prove this last point. There exists, as an after-study to his well-known *Hand of God*, a plaster cast of his own hand holding a little figure which he had earlier modeled. The hand cast from life is exact and complete to every wrinkle and infinitesimal scar. But it is repugnant to both touch and sight, a little like the detached hand of a corpse. The small sculptured figure held in the hand is modeled in a very sketchy fashion and is, from a scientific point of view, a very inaccurate and incomplete reproduction of actual human appearance. But it is charged with warmth and charm, its living quality enhanced by the very contrast which should work, as many might think, to its disadvantage.

Our reason tells us that the limits between the structure of organic forms and sculpture are definite. There is a difference not only of material in this case but of process of formation. The forms of sculpture do not grow organically and slowly from within from infinitesimally small living elements. They are shaped rapidly, often violently, by blows or pressure from without. The blows or pressures are exerted by the hand of a man, and Rodin's study surely reminds us of that fact. Nevertheless, behind this lonely, almost too-scientific experiment, there lies a tradition that associates sculpture with age-old elemental things, with mysterious and fundamental beginnings, where forms in nature and forms in art merge, separate, then once more mingle in men's minds. It takes very little to change the design from a study of the hand of the sculptor to the *Hand of God*, rising from a block of weathered stone. The history of sculpture can show remote and strange examples of hands with figures in their grasp, like certain votive objects of the Greco-Roman Dionysiac cult of Zeus-Sabazios; medieval goldsmiths with their hand-reliquaries forged another link in the chain of formal tradition that leads to the work of Rodin who died hardly more than thirty years ago. Look again and the hand is once more the hand of a man; instead of the hand of a god we find the hand of a sculptor. The poetic spell will work on us too, if we allow our minds to wander in such a maze of associations.

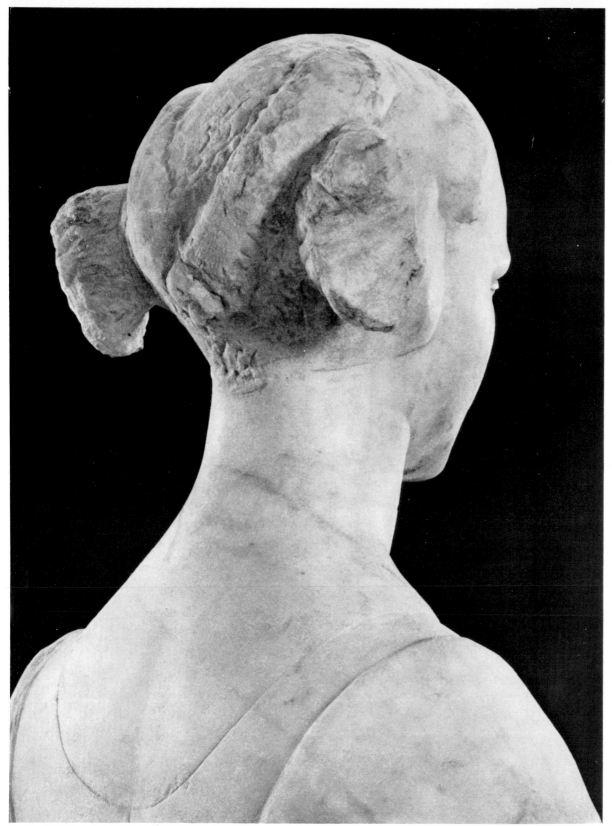

Desiderio da Settignano   *Marietta Strozzi*   Marble
Widener Collection, National Gallery of Art, Washington, D. C.

TWENTY

Even when we are called back from reveries of this sort to reality by considerations of material and technique, the poetic element in sculpture still remains active. For it is impossible to escape completely from the paradoxical relationship of an inner vitality with the inert quality of most materials from which sculpture is made. Sculpture reveals clearly the ambiguous double substance of plastic art, composed on the one hand of inorganic material, eternally lifeless in the biological sense, and, on the other, of an endless life suggested by the art with which that material was shaped. Certain materials seem to determine certain techniques and certain forms. The active principles behind these relationships of material, technique and form define a new source of order and progression. Here too are found vitality and life.

The creation alone of sculpture is not in itself an end. Sculpture enters new phases of life when it leaves the studio of the artist. Time, corrosion, even some breakage, add richness to surfaces, new quality to design. Sculpture also in an active sense interprets our environment and makes a new environment once it takes its place in the world of nature and of men. Created by men, sculpture is one of the means by which each generation of men creates its own world. Those worlds, provided art remains, linger on long after the generation that made them is gone. The past merges in them with the present. From this last poetic ambiguity, concerned with the largest elements of time, emerge the forces of tradition and experiment, seeming opposites, but destined for collaboration.

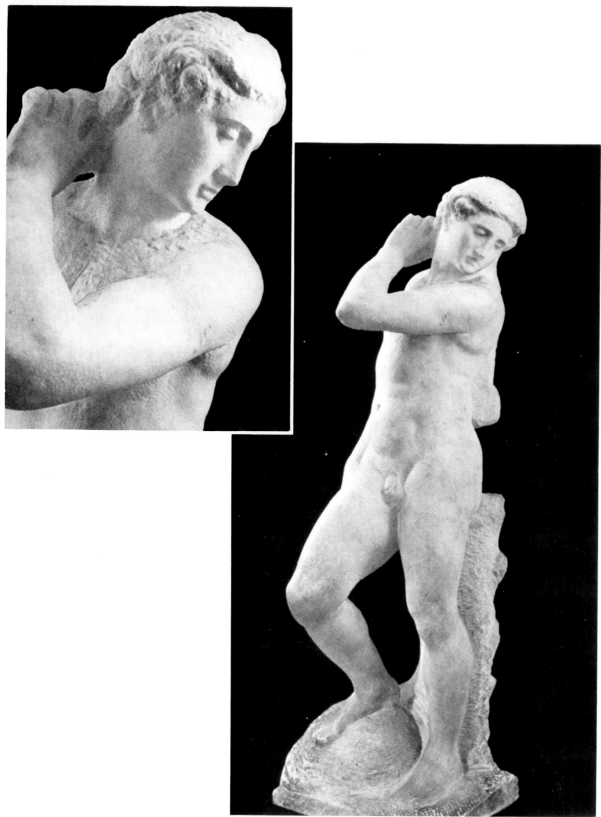

Michelangelo
Museo Nazionale, Florence

David-Apollo   Marble
Courtesy National Gallery of Art

TWENTY-TWO

BACKGROUNDS OF MODERN SCULPTURE

Modern Western sculpture, that is to say, the sculpture of the Western world since 1900, is subject to principles of self-definition and continuity. It contains elements which originated in the past and elements of innovation which belong to the modern world. Both kinds of elements mingle. The work of no one artist, or group of artists, is truly representative of an age; the conservative work side by side with the innovators. But I believe that the leaders, not the rank and file, are the ones whom we should single out for study if we are to sense the life and vigor of an artistic movement. This demands subjective choice and judgments of value which must necessarily be personal. The remarks which follow are not intended as a survey of the whole field, and are based on personal preferences, interests and accident of experience and knowledge at a known risk of error of omission.

Let us put ourselves for a moment in the position of sculptors who were at work, or just beginning to work fifty years ago at the beginning of the 20th century. Two movements or currents of style were in strong evidence, one in particular already in the drying-out stage of academicism. This latter we may call the Humanist tradition stemming from the remainder of late Antique Mediterranean art, certain aspects of medieval art and above all from the classical and realist revival of the Renaissance.

The hallmark of the Humanist tradition was a set of magnificent compromises: compromise between naturalism and the ideal, between the human and the absolute. Its triumph was the creation of a moving and admirable definition of man which in the free-standing figure and portrait-bust was a symbol of freedom. The semi-realistic, semi-idealized figure of man, a combination of the material and the ideal, of brute matter and divinity, was the measure of all things. Note well that this image of man was constructed from a sure knowledge of the human body beneath the outer surface. This was a means of suggesting an inner vitality, as well as a method to preserve a compromise between human form in

Bernini   *Louis XIV*   Marble (Detail)
                    Courtesy Musée de Versailles

TWENTY-FOUR

nature and in the ideal. The procedure is clearly illustrated by Michelangelo's sculpture and even more so, later, by Houdon's painstakingly accurate anatomical study (*écorché*) for his *Saint John the Baptist.*

There is a painting by Boilly of Houdon's studio done toward 1800 which could equally well be called a portrait of the Western Humanist tradition in sculpture just before it entered upon a phase of desiccation in the official schools. The human figure is the focus. The standing figure of the

Detail of opposite plate

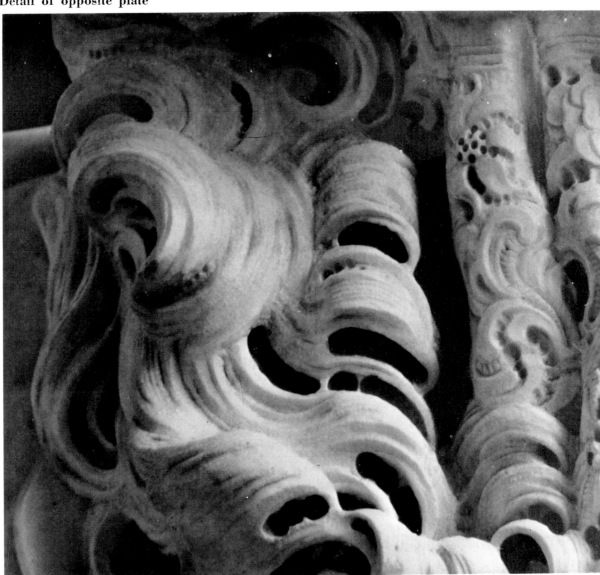

sculptor is in the center of the canvas, and a nude model holds the stage immediately to the right of the artist. In addition, study from life is to be corrected and recast in the forms of the Antique; a plaster cast of a fragmentary Greco-Roman goddess stands for that purpose in the right corner. The background is filled with completed figures; the running *Diana*, the seated *Voltaire*, the famous study-figure of the muscle-man or *écorché* (for the *Saint John*); behind, the portrait busts of contemporary great men, row on row of materialized human dignity and worth, on the shelves above.

Developing as an off-shoot of this extreme, and optimistic, view of human value in sculpture was a livelier and more emotional movement of the 19th century. It passed through the Romantic and painterly genius of Rude, Barye, and above all Carpeaux, to Rodin. And with Rodin it too reached its limits. Whether we call it late Romanticism or Impressionism or just Rodinism, its achievements and failures remain the same. This was above all a visual art of sculpture, of forms defined by ragged silhouette and by picturesque surface modeling at the expense of volumes. To this discipline, or lack of discipline in the contemporary sense, the calm massing of classical sculpture, or indeed of the Humanist tradition, were torn and wind-swept by a kind of gale of the emotions. The definition of man (who still remains the primary object of study and expression) becomes a question of dynamics, of change. The solution of the relation of sculpture to its environment is either one of shock in contrast, or by the application of painterly precepts, that is, by conceiving sculpture as primarily a two-dimensional impression of form merged in a single view with nature, just as a painter merges his figures with their visual surroundings in a picture-scene. Such at least was the avowed and published aim of the Impressionism of Medardo Rosso.*

This obviously was no solution to the problem of sculpture's being in three dimensions. Nor was the painterly handling of lights and darks and the insistence on contour and silhouette at the expense of relief

---

*See R. Goldwater, ed. *Artists on Art*, New York, Pantheon Press, 1941, p. 325.

Rodin   *Age of Bronze*   (Detail)
            Simpson Collection, National Gallery of Art, Washington, D. C.

and constructional modeling. Even so, the Age of Rodin ended with more
than negative results. Rodin proved that European sculpture could be
freed from the moribund tradition of the schools and brought into the
stream of tradition of great creative art of all times and all periods. He
once more brought Western sculpture back to its epic sweep, and made it
a major expression in art in the public mind. He left two formal precepts
which have to do with spatial and environmental aspects and have had a
great deal of influence on modern sculpture: the "block-aesthetic"—whereby the form and marble character of the original stone block is retained

TWENTY-SEVEN

Rodin   *Mouvement de Danse*   Pencil and Wash Drawing
Simpson Collection, National Gallery of Art, Washington, D. C.

TWENTY-EIGHT

Rodin
Villa des Brillants, Meudon, France

Mouvement de Danse   Plaster
Courtesy, Musée Rodin, Paris

TWENTY-NINE

in the finished work as we saw it in the marble *Hand of God*, a revival of an aesthetic of Michelangelo; and the "fragment-aesthetic"—whereby the representational elements of the finished work are daringly cut down, or eliminated, for purposes of expressive design. Finally, Rodin's late experimental work, just before and during three years of the 1914-1918 war, explored possibilities and attitudes toward sculpture which appear today essentially modern. It was the Rodin of the late period whom the older sculptors of our generation knew, and in many cases, worked with.

A First Phase: Bridge Between Eras

The writings, conversations and work of the first generation of 20th-century sculptors reveal clearly how much they owed to Rodin's example and how acutely they felt at the same time the need to strike out for themselves. Maillol said of Rodin: "Rodin is the great genius who has given movement to his whole epoch; he is a man I could never be . . ." Then he added of Rodin, "He understood nothing of medium because he did not cut stone . . . He was too inclined to limit himself to a sketch. He modeled an old woman, reproducing all the wrinkles of her belly. An old woman's belly does not fascinate me: I like health and beauty."

"Health and Beauty." There are the touchstones of Maillol's superb and optimistic rebuilding of the Western tradition. Where he seems most academic it is because his search led him back to the Humanist aesthetic, among the other sources he drew upon. He is a link with an earlier age in more ways than one. Maillol did not devote himself entirely to sculpture until he was forty years old. Before then he was a painter and tapestry designer, primarily. His painting drew upon Renoir and the Symbolist phase of Gauguin, and like Renoir he knew and loved the art of Versailles. From Girardon's nymph reliefs at Versailles Maillol evolved at least one painting, using the same motives, but simplifying and

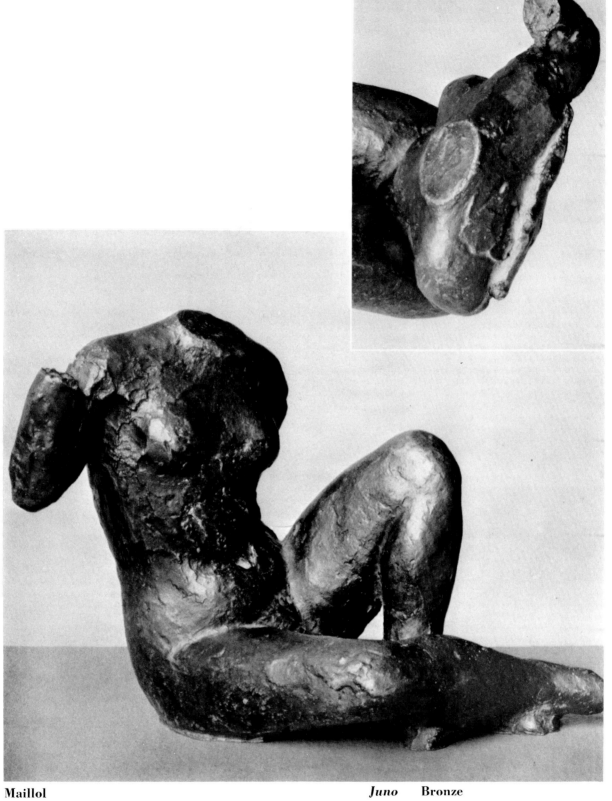

Maillol *Juno* Bronze
Collection of Mr. and Mrs. Andrew S. Keck, Washington, D. C.

Renoir   *Mother and Child* (Detail) Bronze
The Phillips Gallery, Washington, D. C.

patterning the form as much as he constructed. Renoir, in his *Bathers* of 1887 in the Tyson Collection, used the same theme and the same traditional source. But how far superior is Renoir's painting to Maillol's. Maillol's painting is the colored drawing of a sculptor. His true vocation was sculptural, just as Renoir's was in painting. And this is proved by Renoir's own sculpture, like the charming group of his wife and child which is modeled with touches almost like those of the brush, so clearly in the painterly tradition of Carpeaux, yet so deeply infused with Renoir's own healthy delight in human nature that we find in his painting.

There is a clear relation of spirit here with Maillol. But Maillol's sculpture worked toward weight and density and a sense of everlasting strength and stability. His images were generalized. His carving was an act of purification. It was an almost eerie process of purging all the vivid emotion and particularity and flutter in Rodin. *The Mediterranean*, dated 1901, is a landmark to remember. Beneath the full forms in full repose is a geometric pattern of unyielding precision. It is a return from the pole of painting in sculpture toward the abstract architectonic pole. And it is also, in spite of the obvious break from Rodin and its experimental qualities, a return to traditional sources, primarily the great Greek masterpieces of the early 5th century. Here is the same definition of Mediterranean light as a force of Olympian calm and space as a volume in its own right, pressing up unyieldingly against the forms in stone.

There is a danger in pigeonholing both artists and influences. What should concern us most here are the differences between Maillol and the sculpture of Olympia. Roger Fry in his *Last Lectures* dwelt briefly on this very point and noted that Maillol's surfaces and textures and rhythmic repetitions of form disclose a more vivid sensibility than that shown by the Greek sculptors of Olympia.* We can go further now, for example, with his charming early statuette called *Leda*, which by the play of gesture and axes in the design captures quite an un-Greek sense of movement, while still retaining a full measure of stability. This is, of course, a personal achievement, but these characteristics of surface sensibility and movement are clearly inherited by Maillol from the tradition of the 19th century, which in turn depends upon that of 18th-century France and ultimately on Bernini and Michelangelo. And in one portrait-head in particular, so classical and yet with a so great a difference in spiritual awareness, Maillol

---

*Roger Fry, *Last Lectures*, published posthumously, New York-Cambridge, 1939, p. 197.

THIRTY-THREE

Maillol   *Leda*   Bronze
Collection of Hon. and Mrs. Francis Biddle, Washington, D. C.

THIRTY-FOUR

seems to bring to life again that strange and fleeting combination of psychological intensity and strong monumental form of Gothic cathedral sculpture of the 13th century.

This comparison with an architectural sculpture-style of the past cannot be pushed too far. The 20th century, and Maillol is no exception, has had one of its chief difficulties in dealing with architectural sculpture, that is to say the organic incorporation of sculpture into architecture. The most frequent solution has been to affix a figure on the plane surfaces employed by modern architecture as if the sculpture were an enormous seal. The figure adheres to, but does not grow from, the architecture. In fact it appears as a fragment torn from some other function. Rodin had the same difficulty. His *Thinker* looks best alone outside the architectural setting for which it was first conceived. I personally feel a somewhat similar lack of ease in Maillol's case in statuary consisting of a complete figure. The head of Maillol's great *Venus* and the string of beads are strangely incongruous with the simplicity and power of the torso. In bronze and set against a leafy background the effect is better, but stagey and somehow unreal.* The *Venus* is most at home in the artist's studio, and I feel its forms at a more eloquent pitch in a version where the full simplicity of the design is brought out without the arms and head. Sometimes it appears that Maillol went further back than the Greeks, to the Egyptians. There is a chord struck between a plaster torso of his done less than twenty years ago and a fragmentary masterpiece preserved from the reign of Ikhnaton over three thousand years ago. Maillol meets an unknown predecessor as he moves from nature toward abstraction as the Egyptian in the opposite direction moves from abstraction toward nature.

Maillol's portraiture is the least important aspect of his work, but there is a rugged honesty and love in his bronze head of Renoir. Our great American sculptor, Lachaise, reveals an affinity with Maillol's liberating and penetrating style in his portrait of John Marin. The greatest

*See the interesting photograph published in J. Rewald, *Maillol*, London-Paris-New York, 1929, p. 63.

Lachaise   *Portrait of John Marin*   Bronze
Collection of Mr. and Mrs. Andrew S. Keck, Washington, D. C.

THIRTY-SIX

Despiau   *Portrait of Mrs. Edward Bruce*   Bronze
Collection of Mrs. Edward Bruce, Washington, D. C.

portraitist of the 20th century, and perhaps also the most sensitive of all the figure sculptors in a quiet and unobtrusive style, is Despiau, like Maillol dead within the last few years. His is a more humanist art, profoundly versed in the French tradition, as is revealed by his portrait of Madame Derain, which is related in style to that of Mrs. Edward Bruce. The plaster model of the head of Madame Derain in The Phillips Gallery is so subtle that it seems to defy analysis. The closed eyes are a daring flouting of convention, and yet they recall an Oriental tradition of the masks of Buddha or the death masks used in portrait sculpture in an earlier European age. With its mood of calm and introspection, there is still a contrasting life in the modeling which lends it a strange and disturbing unbalance between complete Nirvana and the breath of active emotion and intellect. It is universal and yet particular. Of such elusive values, bound by such bold and perfectly sure definition of forms, is made the poetry of early 20th-century sculpture.

Before moving on to another phase of development in modern Western sculpture I want to suggest also the quality of poetic eloquence in two modern German sculptors. The first, Lehmbruck, grew directly out of Maillol's early experimental work but rapidly developed a personal style of melancholy charm and haunting grace. He turns Maillol's more or less confident classicism to a Romantic nostalgia. Lehmbruck represents what might be called the mannerist phase of Maillol's classicism. More dependent on the medieval tradition is the work of the sculptor Barlach. His figure called *Compassion* recalls the grief-figures of medieval tomb sculpture. One feels an affinity with traditional folk-art in Barlach which makes the medieval archaism somehow legitimate and fresh with sincerity. Barlach's style is interesting for the study of contemporary sculpture because he appears consciously to have explored what might be called negative masses, that is to say voids. His modeling is often by indented planes, as if resulting from the hollow gouge used for wood carving, and in his *Singing Man* the volume of air between the knee, the lap and the torso is of supreme importance to the design. Without it the unity of

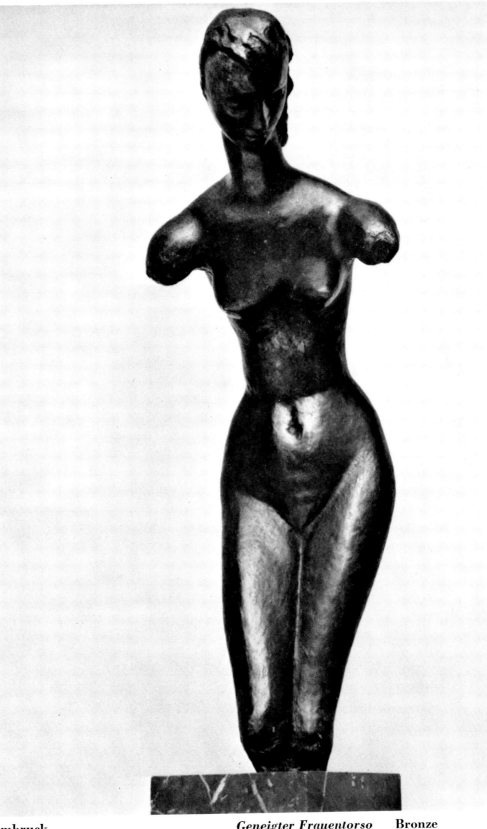

Lehmbruck   *Geneigter Frauentorso*   Bronze
Collection of Mr. and Mrs. Andrew S. Keck, Washington, D. C.

THIRTY-NINE

form, which does exist, can hardly be explained. This is, of course, far removed in spirit from French classicism, and there are strong Romantic overtones in Barlach's *Singing Man* who so wholeheartedly gives his being to a peasant's folk song. One feels the song is momentary, but that the sculptural design is eternal in its geometric balance. Here arises a kind of tingling tension.

Several of the characteristics of style we have noted in this early 20th-century revolt against sculptural "Impressionism" are of great importance to more recent experimental developments. The failure to achieve, as in medieval or Baroque art, a true fusion between architecture and sculpture is one of these. Difficulty in creating homogeneous statuary design thus accentuating the "fragment-aesthetic" left as a legacy by Rodin is another. The "fragment-aesthetic" was also intensified by sympathetic study of older sculpture of very remote periods, like early Greek or even Egyptian sculpture existing by 1900 chiefly as fragments. To the "block-aesthetic" which emphasizes the material point of departure and the inherent formal life of sculpture as opposed to literal imitation of natural forms was added a conscious investigation of space as a volume, and sculptural form began to be thoroughly sensed as consisting of both solids and voids. In this respect Western sculpture began once again to assume a role of monumental interpretation of physical light and above all space. Western sculpture became less a matter of sight and more a matter of touch.

Recognition of this shift toward the sense of touch in Western sculpture can hardly be overemphasized. It appears as a major break with the immediate past and as a sudden and no less dramatic occurrence. Actually there was considerable preparation during the late 19th-century, and the direct implications can hardly be said to have become really evident until 1924, when Brancusi made his classic egg form, entitled *Sculpture for the Blind*. One 19th-century prototype of this tactile approach with insistence on the texture of stone is William Rimmer's portrait head in The Corcoran Gallery of Art, in Washington, of which a reproduction is

Barlach   *Singing Man*   Bronze (Cast #1)
Collection of Mr. and Mrs. Andrew S. Keck, Washington, D. C.

Rimmer   *Head of a Woman*   Granite
The Corcoran Gallery of Art, Washington, D. C.

FORTY-TWO

given here. Degas' sculpture is only superficially related to Rodin's painterly style. In comparison with his own painting Degas' bronzes have a strangely elemental, almost "primitive" quality. Use of real cloth for his standing *Dancer's* dress finds precedent in the popular votive religious images of Europe from the Middle Ages to our own time; it is also reminiscent of real hair or fibers used in Micronesian and African ceremonial masks. The early 20th-century change from visual to tactile approach in sculpture is illustrated by Matisse's progression from his Rodinesque *Serf*.

What of the world created by that generation of sculptors? It is hard to recognize that world today, and in point of fact it is not entirely homogeneous. From Maillol we have a vision of Mediterranean warmth and classic poise — a world of gentle breezes, a place where both the 20th century and the Golden Age of Attica might live together, a fertile world with a rational underlying design and a surface rich with natural gifts, in which man and nature could come to terms favorable to both. It is not a Christian world in the traditional sense, nor is it a world under the confident, individualist domination of the Humanists. Man tends to disappear in favor of woman, who in turn loses individual humanity to become something like the ancient classical personifications of nature—Tellus or Terra, Mother Earth, Venus, the dryads and the hamadryads, the sea-nymphs.

From the German sculptors, less deeply imbued with the Latinity of France, there comes a greater sense of urgency and apprehension, a greater willingness to elongate, to distort the human figure to express a fragile, more momentary existence in a more mysterious and more menacing environment. This vision is, however, like the French if only because it carries with it a sense of nostalgia. And in fact this sculpture in total does not appear today to create a whole world so much as isolated compartments, islands of feeling, within the larger world of human living rushing into a new age.

Wooden Masks, Ivory Coast, Africa
Smithsonian Institution, United States National Museum, Washington, D. C.

FORTY-FOUR

Degas   *Dancer*   Bronze

The Baltimore Museum of Art

Rodin   *The Walking Man*   Bronze
Simpson Collection, National Gallery of Art, Washington, D. C.

FORTY-SIX

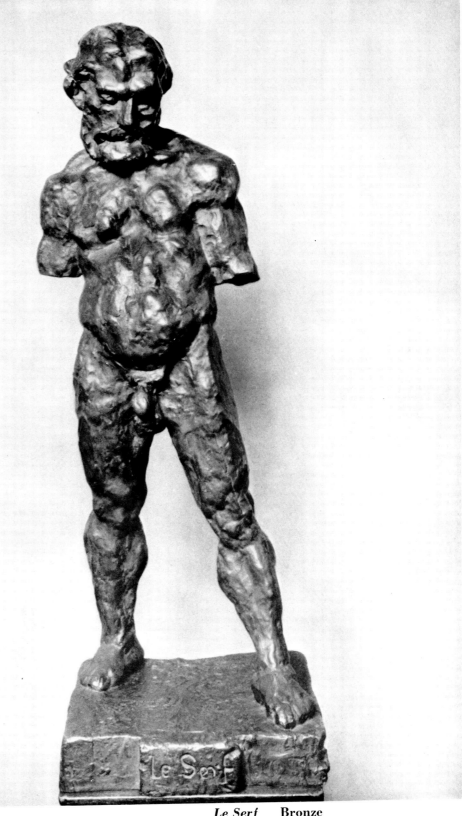

Matisse   *Le Serf*   Bronze
The Cone Collection, The Baltimore Museum of Art

FORTY-SEVEN

Matisse   *Tiari With a Necklace*   Bronze
The Cone Collection, The Baltimore Museum of Art

FORTY-EIGHT

Matisse   *Venus on the Shell*   Bronze
The Cone Collection, The Baltimore Museum of Art

A Second Phase: Sculpture of the Machine Age

Toward 1900 the American philosopher and historian, Henry Adams, became concerned with the action of tradition and experiment within this larger world, as he saw it, of human living. Adams saw the traditional combination of Western humanistic religion and laws of human nature as force which he called the Virgin, and particularly the Virgin of Chartres. He saw the Virgin at grips with a new force, a new source of power, largely modern physics, expressed in the man-made machine or the Dynamo. He called his time a time of crisis, and he predicted the ultimate victory of the Dynamo.*

My final observations deal with Adams' vision of the Dynamo and its implications and apparent effects as we can see them in modern sculpture. One might think that the art of the Machine Age would be by definition entirely experimental. Is not recent applied physics, the Dynamo as Adams called it, completely modern? Are not our physical theories of energy and indeed of the mechanics of the universe different from past theories? What possible source of tradition would have relevance to our machine-age sculpture? Actually, tradition still remains in interplay with experiment, but with the significant difference that the artistic traditions formerly at work have been exchanged for traditions originating in other sources.

A large part of the unusual and apparently cryptic aspects of machine-age sculpture is in the fact that the traditions most nearly approaching, and in some cases, deliberately utilized by the sculptors of the very recent past come not from Renaissance proto-scientific or mechanic sources (i.e. Leonardo da Vinci) but from cultures extremely remote from the use and development of machinery as we know it in our modern civilization. It is true nevertheless that certain effects of the machine were at first, well before the war of 1914-1918, expressed in sculpture in terms of

---

*See in particular *The Education of Henry Adams* as well as *Mont Saint-Michel and Chartres.*

non-naturalistic forms, not unlike the forms of machinery itself. And these forms were given a marked suggestion of movement. Here is a fundamentally differing expression than the forms chosen by Maillol, where the dynamics are conceived as entirely nature-born and so expressed. To sense this difference directly, compare Maillol's relief, *Desire*, with the relief called the *Lovers*, by Duchamp-Villon, dated 1913.[1] In the latter the forms of nature, broken down and reduced to design-symbols of speed, are set in motion, and rush one group toward the other like steel filings to a magnet. A classic example of this tendency toward abstraction involving motion is Brancusi's reduction of a natural phenomenon of great beauty, the flight of a bird, to a single, streamlined jet. It was also possible for Brancusi to modify this design in subtle ways to suggest a momentary arrest of motion.[2] A similar reduction of natural human forms to complex geometric shapes is apparent in the portrait-bust, incidentally built up on a program of Western traditional sculpture, of *Mlle. Pogany* by Brancusi. Here, also, the polished metal version is the more eloquent; its dynamics seem to work more smoothly and with less friction both in material and technique.[3] One could multiply examples of novel forms growing out of the use of new metals and substances like plastics which have played so important a role in the recent break from the 19th century in sculpture.

With these few instances alone, there appear to be the makings for an expression in sculpture that belongs to the age of the airplane, the streamliner and to other mechanistic aspects of the 20th century as we have come, to our peril as well as to our advantage, to it. Most interesting, however, is the fact that what might be termed machinery-forms occur in the sculpture of many very old, so-called "primitive" cultures. There are

---

[1] Both in the Museum of Modern Art, New York.

[2] Examples of the *Bird*, in flight and at rest, in varying materials are in this country in some number: for example Dreier and Arensberg Collections and Museum of Modern Art.

[3] An example in stone in the Arensberg Collection; a version in polished metal in the Norton Gallery of Art (Ralph H. Norton Collection, West Palm Beach).

Wooden Mask, Upper Ivory Coast, West Africa
Smithsonian Institution, United States National Museum, Washington, D. C.

FIFTY-TWO

Brancusi   *The Princess*   Polished bronze on a stone base
Louise and Walter Arensberg Collection, Hollywood, California

FIFTY-THREE

Puerto Rican Stone Collar and Zemes
Smithsonian Institution United States National Museum, Washington, D. C.

animal-forms in American Indian sculpture which are extremely close to the principles underlying Brancusi's abstractions. There are surprising analogies between certain Puerto Rican sculptures in stone, of as yet uncertain date and function, and the devices of contemporary Western sculptors in the use of voids as dominant features of design and the alteration

FIFTY-FOUR

Brancusi   *The Fish*   Marble on round mirror
Louise and Walter Arensberg Collection, Hollywood, California

of organic natural forms.[4]   The causes of these particular correspondences are not clear although other close correspondences between the work of our contemporary sculptors since 1900 and many aspects of African and Oriental sculpture can be accounted for on the basis of historically substantiated influences.

What seems most important is a general formal affinity which parallels, rather than strictly depends from, modern scientific developments. The recent "discovery" of exotic arts, pre-Hellenic arts or folk-arts by Western artists, somewhat after those arts were known to antiquarians, archeologists and anthropologists, must correspond to definite needs on the part of contemporary sculptors growing from their own experimental work. Where they have sought for freedom from the Humanist tradition they have found the support of arts untouched by the stamp of their own immediate traditional past.   Faced with the perplexities, confusion and contradictions of modern society, contemporary sculptors appear to seek out the deepest reservoirs of the race's collective experience.   A large part of the appeal of these exotic arts is in the clear enunciation of basic sculptural principles: of forms completely felt as a whole in the round, of well defined planes, of subtle and exciting relationships of forms in a design.   It is significant, nevertheless, for the general problem of relationship between experiment and tradition that contemporary Western emphasis on the creation of a new art in sculpture from intense experiment has brought out affinities with arts in which tradition is far stronger than in any phase of style developed up to the present by Western civilization.   It would appear that experiment is impelled to search out and find a corresponding counterweight in tradition, even if the traditions in point are on the surface extremely remote in time and geography and "layer" of civilization.

Our Western world today, insofar as it is created by art, is a mixture of many periods of style and many conflicting aims.   An artist's vision of this world is by no means what we see about us.   The effects of two world

---

[4] Examples in the Smithsonian Collection, United States National Museum.

wars have without doubt been a devastating deterrent. Sculpture's part, particularly in relation to architecture, has been dwindling. No sculptural form could do much but detract from the clean planes of modernist architecture. As far as one can judge, the formal trend of modern architecture is austere and rational and yet concerned with a kind of beauty which is far from utilitarian in its effects. The much-used word "functional" covers a multitude of effects which seem sheerly beautiful. The recent exhibition in the Museum of Modern Art in New York of the work of the architect, Mies van der Rohe, indicated to me that perhaps the poetic vision rather than the function of a modern building is the important element.* Or at least I was made to feel that the idea of function was first of all poetry before being utility or practicality. Such certainly were Mies van der Rohe's visions of form in the transparent material of glass (1921).

Such visionary architecture is related to constructions in transparent and semi-transparent materials in which the sculpture of Gabo or Pevsner take their form. The work of Gabo suggests an interesting phenomenon. Architecture no longer is able to assimilate sculpture as part of its organic design—and in fact has found increasing use of the alphabetic letter or word in block-letters for plastic and intellectual characterization. These letters move over the boundary between sign and form and take the place of traditional monumental sculpture. Sculpture, set free, has begun to assume the qualities of architecture itself. It becomes less a solid with representational values than an abstract construction with voids and solids interplaying. One can begin to speak concerning this "constructional" sculpture, as of architecture, of exterior masses and interior space. Cables used in suspension bridges appear as strings or wires in abstract sculpture to express tension. One must also recognize in many of these sculptural constructions a character of a portable object as well as relationships with such beautiful and formally interesting objects as stringed musical instruments, familiar in the "iconography" of Cubism.

---

*See the excellent illustrated catalogue by P. C. Johnson, Museum of Modern Art, N. Y., 1947.

Gabo   *Linear Construction, Variations*   Plastic
The Phillips Gallery, Washington, D. C.

The rationale of the modern spirit has had certain poetic consequences which bear directly on the role of the sculpture of our day. The urge toward order finds expression in the re-making of urban environment where simple clearly defined geometric forms can be inserted, in project at least, within the tattered confusion of the 19th-century utilitarian city. Art under this principle could express, toward 1920 and for a time thereafter, an antagonism to nature.[1] And in imagination, as some modern painting reveals, ordered shapes, like colossal abstract sculptural forms, can even be conceived as invading the countryside.[2] But at this point there comes into evidence a counter-movement which restores a balance, bringing into play relationships with nature and with them poetical values of the highest order.[3]

At no time within the past three hundred years has the natural world of plants and trees, of the good earth and mountains and boulders, of clear air and sunlight been so prized as at the present. One thinks of traditional Japanese domestic architecture in looking at some modern domestic interiors, where the walls are removed in favor of glass and interior and exterior space seem to merge. The world of nature, out-of-doors, has as great, or a greater, role to play than man-made construction. At least the severe rigidity of the lines and planes of modernist architecture—the "machine for living" in Corbusier's phrase—seem to attract as compensation the richness and accidental details in views of nature. Sculpture has its place in this poetic economy, as an accent, as a scale-giving index, as a link between man and nature. But its forms are likely to be in harmony with other environments than architecture and with other forces than human rationality.

---

[1] "A city! . . . It is the grip of man upon nature. It is a human operation directed against nature . . . ." Le Corbusier, ed. in English translation, *The City of Tomorrow and its Planning*, London, John Rokker, 1929, p. xxi.

[2] For example Magritte's imagery; see his *Mental Calculus* (1931) reproduced in *Art in Our Time*, Museum of Modern Art, N. Y., 1939, p. 193.

[3] On this phenomenon see Henry-Russell Hitchcock, *Painting toward Architecture*, Duell, Sloan and Pearce, N. Y., 1948, pp. 26-30, 40-44.

Lipschitz   *Sacrifice*   Bronze
Buchholz Gallery, New York

Zapotec Funerary Urn, State of Oaxaca, Mexico.   Fired Clay
Smithsonian Institution, United States National Museum, Washington, D. C.

The images by the influential sculptor, Lipschitz, are frequently combinations of human forms and machine forms, and yet in surface they suggest the tooling not by modern machinery but by the patient craftsmanship of the Bronze Age. More important, they often suggest an idol, a fearsome object possessed of a spirit which in some way, we know not how, or by what rites, must be propitiated. One must go to African

Bronze Tiger, Chinese, Chou Dynasty 1122-255 B.C.
Courtesy Smithsonian Institution, Freer Gallery of Art, Washington, D. C.

SIXTY-TWO

Marini   *Cavaliere*   Bronze
             Buchholz Gallery, New York

Images on outer slope of Rano Raraku, Easter Island
Courtesy American Museum of Natural History, New York

Negro sculpture or far back, perhaps as far as Neolithic times, to find a parallel subjection of the human figure to such haunting abstraction of nature and natural forces.

The poetics of sculpture like that of Henry Moore are related. These are forms which have ambiguous associations, partly a reference to the machine-forms of our own civilization partly a reference to the natural "sculpture" of boulders and trees in nature. They make a powerful appeal to the sense of touch and exploit in far more direct ways than did Maillol, for one example, with contours and spatial volumes, fuller possibilities of sculpture as defined in physical space and light. Their strangeness to many of us is such that they seem to be foreign apparitions from another world. In Moore's drawings his figures often appear in imaginary landscapes suggesting by a detail here, or an intimation there, some remote environment accessible to the mind and spirit rather than to our physical being. But there are landscapes with sculpture which recall his world. Following W. R. Valentiner *(Origins of Modern Sculpture, 1946)*, one can cite distant Easter Island in the Pacific, or closer to his own studio in England, the old Druidic groves of stones in Cornwall or Brittany. Such is at least part of his tradition, as are certain medieval forms derived from the sculptor's wide knowledge of the English and European Continental past.

Moore's poetry most clearly evokes the mysteries of fundamental origins available in sculpture and plays upon the poetic ambiguity that his stone is not a sculptor's stone but a boulder washed by the rain, that the image is no man-made image but a fantasy wrought by a divinity that lives in the wind and makes his presence known in the storm. The contours of his sculpture when they do not suggest the action of machinery, suggest more than anything else a magical erosion. We can feel his sculp-

Images from Easter Island
Courtesy American Museum of Natural History, New York

Angel in Bronze Italian, XII century
Walters Art Gallery, Baltimore

SIXTY-SIX

Moore *Family Group* Bronze
The Phillips Gallery, Washington, D. C.

ture as a part of a great natural unity, pursuing its way heedless of man's will or abilities, as in Wordsworth's words,

Roll'd round in earth's diurnal course,
With rocks, and stones, and trees.

These affinities make this kind of sculpture difficult to place in man-made surroundings. This type of sculpture, this kind of aesthetic, seem to require a natural setting rather than a background of skyscrapers or factories. One is tempted to think of Calder's "mobile" sculpture in the open air near grass and trees, where the chance movement of a breeze sets it into haphazard changing patterns like the shifting patterns caused by the wind in branches and foliage. And many a design in stone by perhaps the most talented and regretted of modern American sculptors, Flannagan, demands the natural setting which its forms insistently emphasize. The poetry of one of his sculptures play between the inert geology of a boulder and the calcified organic structure of an egg; between the duration of eons of time in rock and the moment of awakening life, which already in a flash sinks back into the suggestion of death, becomes assimilated into the lasting forms of natural continuity. This concept occurs often in his animal sculpture.

Although he reveals his grounding in European tradition in his sense of free will, and in his feeling for compassion, Flannagan was much influenced by Aztec sculpture of the Pre-Columbian period. Increasing sympathy on the part of contemporary Western artists for that richly plastic art, as well as African Negro art only a little earlier, has been touched on. As a corollary to the attraction of forms and the very weight of tradition in such arts, as discussed above, we can hardly fail to recognize a contemporary psychological affinity, in particular, for these two distant arts of fearful propitiation, in which the image of man is subjected to a necessity beyond the powers of reason or the control of science; through which, in one, are placated the spirits of the world and of the dead, and, in the other, the blood sacrifice of mankind to the insatiably thirsty gods is perpetually required.

SIXTY-EIGHT

Surely there is no greater contrast than between the sculpture of the Humanist climax of Western civilization and the sculpture of its present state of crisis. In the Renaissance, Michelangelo thought of symbolizing man's subjection of nature and his inherent superiority over his destiny by carving the very marble mountains of Carrara in the colossal images of man. Giovanni da Bologna actually did carve in the gardens of Pratolino a miniature mountain of volcanic tufa in the form of a strong, weathered old man to personify the Apennines. If the Renaissance could change a mountain into man, many of our contemporary sculptors do the opposite. They tend in carving recumbent figures no less poetically to change man into a mountain. And in so doing they seem to call attention to his brief span of life and to a source of strength and power outside his immediate being:

I will lift up mine eyes unto the hills from
whence cometh my help.

Flannagan   *Goat*   Granite
                    The Baltimore Museum of Art

Birth Goddess
Robert Woods Bliss Collection

Mexican, Aztec, c.1450-1500, Aplite
Courtesy National Gallery of Art

SEVENTY

Flannagan   *Kneeling Woman*   Sandstone
Collection of Mr. and Mrs. Andrew S. Keck, Washington, D. C.

Roszak   *Spectre of Kitty Hawk*   **Steel and Bronze**
Owned by the artist

Let us admit the drama of this contrast. At the same time we should recognize that it results not from an arbitrary confrontation of opposites but from a development in a series of actions and reactions which are evident if we but look for them. More than this, Adams' nightmare of a completely material civilization has by no means been borne out by the sculpture of the period of the Dynamo's ascendancy. Let me summarize these findings in another way with four examples chosen from the drawings of sculptors.

David Smith   *Cello Player*   **Steel**
                          Willard Gallery, New York

David Smith   *Insect*   Steel
Willard Gallery, New York

SEVENTY-FOUR

Zapotec Funerary Urn, State of Oaxaca, Mexico, Fired Clay
Smithsonian Institution, United States National Museum, Washington, D. C.

Imagine that you hold in your hands a sheaf of drawings arranged in a rough chronological order. You pick out the first, let us say, by Bouchardon, a French sculptor of great ability of the 18th century. It is clearly an expression of the Humanist tradition—the forms derived from life-studies modified by attentive study of the Greco-Roman Antique. The figure stands out clearly against a background indicated only by abstract shading. This image of humanity refers to a self-sufficient independence. No force can be imagined with more power, more confidence.

The second drawing, by Rodin, moves away from the Humanist tradition, by 1850 already academic. It establishes a more visual, painterly definition of form, caught rapidly in a merging impression, full of a wild, lyrical emotion to which the human figure is subjected and modified. Yet this is still a Humanist expression in so far as the emotional strength seems to rise from within the artist's concept of humanity rather than outside it.

An epitome of the early 20th-century reaction against Rodin may be found in a drawing, let us say, by Despiau. The simple, clear and sensitive line defines a structure by massing. And although we must assume that the drawing was made directly from life, the forms of nature are altered, simplified, arranged and in a way made abstract to bring out more clearly an orderly relationship. If there is a reminiscence of the Antique it is of the pure Greek of the late 6th or early 5th century, uncongenial to the sculptors of an earlier age, and indeed a source made available to the West only by the archaeological research of the 19th and 20th centuries. One does not think of archaeology here but of a chord which brings one short-lived moment of the Western tradition into harmony with a related moment in the Greek tradition.

You may come, finally, to a drawing by Henry Moore. It carries much further the abstract quality of form which we saw suggested by Despiau. It breaks with the remainder of the Humanist tradition in Despiau and sets up a new and very different evaluation of both humanity and man's environment. Yet in this eerie glimpse into another world, who

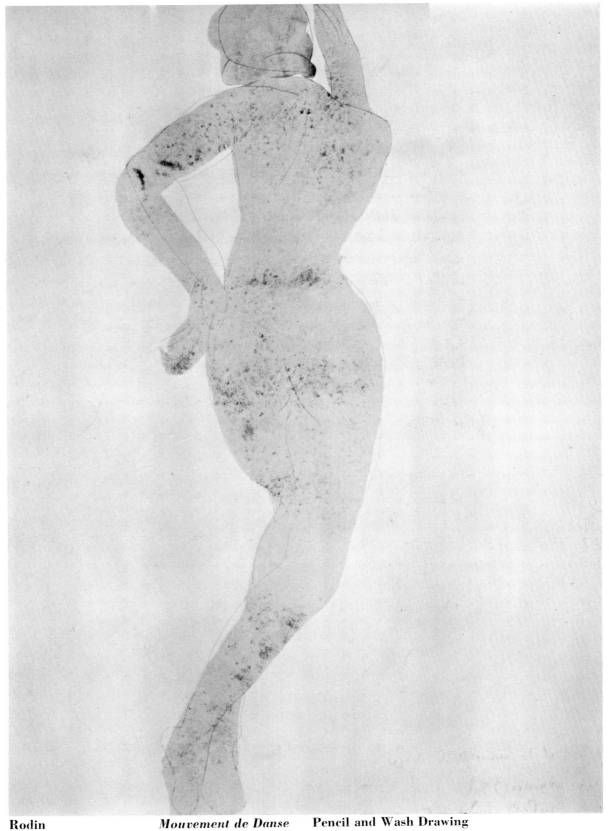

Rodin   *Mouvement de Danse*   Pencil and Wash Drawing
Simpson Collection, National Gallery of Art, Washington, D. C.

SEVENTY-SEVEN

would be bold enough to deny some last vestige of Ancient Mediterranean civilization, altered and distorted to be sure by the influence of more primitive artistic tradition, but subsisting as part of a new and very complex amalgam? Moore's drawing retains a sense of Aristotlean tragedy. Here the protagonist is not an individual but a whole society, a whole way of life, threatened by some as yet dimly perceived catastrophe. It is both an acceptance of, and a protest against, the period we live in. The figures have no specific action. They wait, merely, like granitic ghosts. They exist, in the drawing, not in the real space of every-day life but in a visionary world. Moore's sculpture is as much as ever concerned with problems of reconciling man, nature and man's mechanical techniques;

Moore   *Figures in a Setting*   Drawing
The Phillips Gallery, Washington, D. C.

Enlarged detail of opposite plate

SEVENTY-NINE

Easter Island monolithic image, Volcanic stone
Smithsonian Institution, United States National Museum, Washington, D. C.

EIGHTY

Lilli Gettinger   *Self-Portrait*   Bricks
                    Owned by the artist

Canaanite Figure, Bronze, About 100 B.C.
Walters Art Gallery, Baltimore

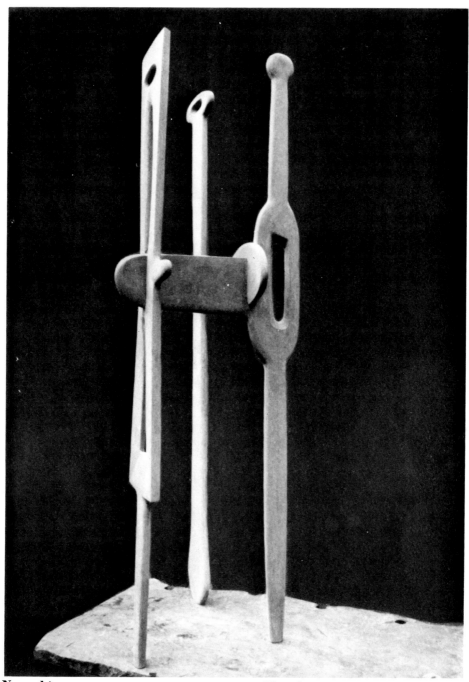

Noguchi   *The Gunas*   Tennessee Marble
Egan Gallery, New York

but he finds new and living forms to express the tensions which Houdon's contemporary, William Blake, poetically symbolized with the "green and pleasant land" of Albion and the machinery of his "mills." Symbols change, largely because their original clarity of meaning is lost or overlaid; the intrinsic meanings of the forms of art remain. Moore rejoins his country-man, Blake, of more than a century earlier, in his insistence upon the vision seen in the spirit's eye.

Thus experiment works with tradition to create eloquence in the language of sculptural forms. By experiment we have meant essentially the search for self-definition. It is the Promethean, fire-giving, life-making, and life-defining element in every work of art. It is the element with which every great artist defines his world. This creative element does not exist

Noguchi *Night Land* York Fossil
Egan Gallery, New York

Blade-shaped carving, Mexican Gulf Coast, Totonac, Basalt
Robert Woods Bliss Collection   Courtesy National Gallery of Art

in a vacuum. It is formed and aided by contact with many forces, among them tradition. Tradition contains the elements of order and continuity. They may be handed down from generation to generation. Or they may rise up from the depths of time to meet and merge with forms created in a similar spirit or at an analogous stage in the development of styles. Tradition in its best sense is a matter of affinities of the human spirit. It destroys the shackling effects of chronological time and sets up a common ground of contact between all artists of all periods belonging to what Henri Focillon called the same "spiritual families." Ossip Zadkine, a contemporary sculptor who certainly cannot be classed as a traditionalist in the usual narrow sense, has spoken of the role of tradition in these words: "There is no past in art, only an exciting present illuminated by the wise smile of the past."

To see experiment and tradition in this way, not as enemies, or as separate entities, but as inseparable forces of the creative process in art, is to recognize one more set of what I have called divergent poles of poetic meaning within sculpture considered as a language of forms. Although we have witnessed since 1900 a break of enormous proportions with the Renaissance and subsequent Humanist tradition in Western sculpture, the elements of tradition and experiment are no less present today than four hundred years ago. Nor is the sculpture of our day in its own way a less expressive element itself in defining a world and an approach to life. Art is a way of knowledge as well as of feeling. Sculpture speaks in metaphor, but it starts and ends with realities.